# TRAVEL DELHI

## Places to Visit in Delhi

BY

SHALU SHARMA

ISBN-13: 978-1507709795
ISBN-10: 150770979X
Publisher: CreateSpace Independent Publishing Platform,
North Charleston, SC

# About the author

Shalu Sharma is travel blogger and enthusiast from India. She was born and brought in the state of Bihar, India. She has lived in India and the UK and travelled extensively around the world with her husband. She has worked as a sales woman, worked for a law firm and nearly ended up as a lecturer in Indian history. Now she just travels when she can and blogs. She has lived and worked in Delhi for several years and continues to visit her relatives and friends there.

Shalu Sharma at the Taj Mahal in Agra

She is the author of many books which can be found on ShaluSharma.Net

Essential India Travel Guide: Travel Tips And Practical Information

India Travel Survival Guide For Women

Essential Hindi Words And Phrases For Travelers To India

Hindi Language For Kids And Beginners: Speak Hindi Instantly

India Travel Health Guide: Health Advice and Tips for Travelers to India

Real Ghost And Paranormal Stories From India

India For Kids: Amazing Facts About India

You can connect with her on her social media sites

Twitter: https://twitter.com/bihar
Google Plus: https://plus.google.com/+ShaluSharma1
Pinterest: http://www.pinterest.com/shalusharma
Facebook: https://www.facebook.com/TourIncredibleIndia

## Introduction

If you are heading off to Delhi and have no idea what to do or places to visit then keep reading. This book contains the top places to visit in Delhi. The book is not meant to be a travel guide but a resource of the best places to visit in Delhi. If you want to make the most of your travel, then this is for you.

For the first time traveller, Delhi can be a noisy, chaotic place that can take anyone out of their comfort zone. Like it or hate it, Delhi is one of the most fascinating places you will ever visit.

This lively place is Karol Bagh Market

Delhi is one of India's most visited cities by foreign tourists not because it is the capital of India but because it is truly a place where they can experience India in its best form. There are so many things to do and places to see.

Once you have arrived in Delhi at the Indira Gandhi International Airport, I suggest you take a few hours of rest at your hotel before your venture out. This will allow you to get rid of the tiredness of the journey and refresh you to enjoy what India has to offer. If you are arriving in the summer, you will find Delhi a very hot place and if you are there in the winter, you will find that it can be very cold particularly in the months of December and January. So dress appropriately.

Remember, Delhi is comprised of Old Delhi and New Delhi. The city of Delhi is an ancient one; it is thought to have been inhabited since the 6th century B.C. It used to be the capital of the Pandavas called the Indraprastha of the great Indian epic the Mahabharata. Many battles have been fought for the city; it has been raided, rebuilt and ransacked multiple times. Astonishing place indeed, just like all great capital cities of the world!

The capital of India is New Delhi; it is here where all the government buildings and embassies are situated. It is basically the seat of the government of India. It is described as the National Capital Territory of India and was designed by Sir Edwin Lutyens during the British Raj to accommodate the shifting of the capital of India from Calcutta to Delhi. You will find high rise buildings, modern infrastructure, big flyovers wide roads, bars, restaurants and shopping malls. Old Delhi was founded by the Mughal

Emperor Shahjahan in the year 1639 and called it Shahjahanabad after his own name. Shahjahanabad and now Old Delhi is a crowded and largely congested place. Although, it is very difficult to define the boundary of Old and New Delhi, you can make it out by the architecture of the buildings.

The best modes of transport in Delhi is the auto-rickshaws, taxis (pre-paid and metered), hired cars from the hotel and the metro. I do not recommend using public transport particularly buses. You can either hire a taxi for the entire day at the hotel though they will charge you more but is a safer option. Alternatively you can go for organised Delhi tours or simply hop in an auto-rickshaw or a taxi and take your own time and see as much or little as you like.

## About this book:

This mini book is about showing the best places to visit in the Indian capital. This is not intended to be a guide but something that will give you ideas on places to visit and things to do on your trip to Delhi. For more information on travelling to India visit ShaluSharma.com.

# Humayun's Tomb

Humayun's Tomb as the name suggests is the tomb or mausoleum of the Mughal Emperor Humayun along with tombs of many other dignitaries of the Mughal Empire. It was built between the years of 1569-70 by his first wife Bega Begum, on the banks of the River Yamuna in Delhi in the memory of her husband. When she died, she was also buried there. The last Mughal emperor Bahadur Shah II was captured here by Lieutenant Hudson in 1857 A.D.

The tomb has been declared as a UNESCO World Heritage Site since 1993. You will find cenotaphs all around the building. To void vandalism, these cenotaphs have been bricked. You will need a good 1 to 2 hours to view and admire the garden and the interiors and exteriors of mausoleum. You will also find the tomb of Isa Khan, an Afghan noble, in the complex.

Address: Mathura Road, New Horizon School, Sundar Nagar, National Capital Region, Nizamuddin, New Delhi, Delhi 110013, India; Phone: +91 11 2435 5275

Fee: 250 Rupees for foreigners.

Humayun's Tomb

# Red Fort

Located in the centre of Delhi, the Red Fort or the Lal Quila (in Hindi) symbolises India and is Delhi's most famous monument and a World Heritage Site. You will find the Indian flag flying from the top of the monument and it is here that the Prime Minister of India hoists the flag from the main gate of the fort on Independence Day and delivers a speech to the nation. It used to be the residence of the Mughal emperors after it was built in 1628-58 by Mughal emperor Shahjahan. There are 3 gates called Lahori Gate (the main gate), Delhi Gate and Water Gate along with lots of other structures, mosques and quarters of the Mughal family. It's a reminder of the magnificent power of the Mughal Empire. You will need at least 2 to 3 hours to explore depending how interesting you find the place. There are organized tours and you can also get a guide. There is a sound and light show in the evening highlighting the events related to the fort in India's history.

Address: Netaji Subhash Marg, Chandni Chowk, New Delhi, Delhi 110006; Phone: +91 11 2327 7705

Fees: 250 Rupees for foreign nationals and free for children up to 15 years.

The Red Fort

# India Gate

India Gate (not to be confused by Gateway of India in Mumbai) was built to commemorate the heroism of the 82,000 Indian soldiers who died in the First World War and the Third Anglo-Afghan War for the British Empire. Originally called the All India War Memorial is located near Rajpath, the boulevard in New Delhi that runs from Rashtrapati Bhavan or Presidents house on Raisina Hill to the National Stadium. You will find that India Gate resembles the architectural style of the triumphal arch of the Arch of Constantine and the Arc de Triomphe de l'Étoile in Paris.

India Gate was commissioned to be built by the Imperial War Graves Commission (IWGC) and completed in 1931. It was designed by designed by Edwin Lutyens, one of the architects of New Delhi.

It is a well maintained monument and you will find the place quite relaxing. There is an ever burning eternal flame of the immortal soldier to respect the fallen soldiers. You can walk around the triumphal arch and read the soldiers names engraved on the gate. Sometimes, the monument is sealed off for political purposes. You will need about 30 minutes to walk around. There is no entry fee.

Address: Rajpath, India Gate, New Delhi 110001

India Gate, World War I memorial in New Delhi

# Rashtrapati Bhavan

The Rashtrapati Bhavan or the Presidential Residence is the official home of the President of India. You might find it funny to visit the resident of the president of India but Rashtrapati Bhavan and the its Mughal Gardens happen to be a popular place to visit in New Delhi. It was originally made to house the British Viceroy when the capital was shifted to Delhi from Calcutta.

You will need permission to visit the president's house by making a booking online on this website: http://presidentofindia.nic.in/visit-to-rashtrapati-bhavan.htm. The opening hours are between 9 am to 4 pm. The visiting days are Fridays, Saturdays and Sundays and not open for visitors from Monday to Thursday and on Indian holidays. Foreign nationals must bring photocopies of their passport.

Address: Rashtrapati Bhavan, New Delhi 110 004. Telephone: 011 - 23013287, 23015321; Email: reception-officer@rb.nic.in

Fees: 25 Rupees

Rashtrapati Bhavan, New Delhi

# Qutab Minar

The Qutab Minar at 100 metres tall is the second tallest minar or minaret in India. The tower is made of red sandstone and marble and is a great looking medieval structure. The building of the monument was initiated by Qutb-ud-din Aibak (hence the name), the sultan of Delhi and completed by Iltutmish and finally by Firoz Shah Tughlaq in 1368. These were all Muslim kings of Turkish descent. It was built to celebrate the victory of the Muslim kings over the defeat of the Hindu Rajput warriors. It is said that the stones and pillars were taken from demolished Hindu temples and was made to serve the purpose of calling for prayers to the faithful.

Address: Mehrauli, New Delhi, Delhi 110030, India; Phone: +91 11 2469 8431

Fees: 250 Rupees for foreigners. You will need about 1 to 2 hours here.

The Qutub Minar: Built to celebrate the defeat of the last Hindu Kingdom of Delhi

# Lodi Gardens

The Lodi (Lodhi) Gardens spread over 90 acres of land is a very popular park in Delhi. It is not just any park or garden, it contains the tomb of Sikander Lodi who happened to be the Sultan of Delhi between the years of 1489 to 1517. Sikandar Lodi was a religious fanatic and had destroyed many Hindu temples and burned alive a Hindu holy man called Bodhan. He also built the last few storeys of the Qutab Minar.

You will find the Lodi Gardens a very beautiful place and a place where you can relax and enjoy the monuments within their gardens. Why not have a picnic there! You will find lots of walkers and joggers taking their morning stroll. If you love gardens then you will like the lovely palm trees and ancient buildings and tombs.

Address: Lodhi Road, close to Khan Market, Prathviraj Road Area, New Delhi, 110003; Phone: +91 11 2464 0079

Fees: No entry fees and opens between 6 am to 7 pm. You will need at least 1 to 2 hours here.

The Sheesh Gumbad at the Lodhi Gardens

# Raj Ghat

The Raj Ghat is a memorial to Mahatma Gandhi, the father of the nation. It is here on this very spot that he was cremated on 31 January 1948, the day after he was assassinated. Built on the banks of the River Yamuna in Old Delhi and surrounded by beautiful gardens, it is another oasis away from the hustle and bustle of Delhi. The actual memorial is built of black marble platform and has a flame on one end that burns all the time.

Within the complex and vicinity there are other memorials of Indian leaders such as that of Indira Gandhi, Sanjay Gandhi, Rajiv Gandhi, Jawaharlal Nehru, Lal Bahadur Shastri and others.

Address: Raj Ghat, New Delhi, 110006

Fees: There are no entry fees. It should take about an hour to pay your respects to the Mahatma and walk around the gardens.

Visitors at the Raj Ghat paying their respects to Mahatma Gandhi

# Birla Mandir Temple (Lakshmi Narayan)

If you are of the spiritual type and want to experience Indian religions then I suggest you check out some of the popular religious destinations of India on my blog. You can read more about basics of the Hindu religion here: http://www.shalusharma.com/hinduism-facts. If you want to visit a Hindu temple then visit the Birla Mandir Temple also known as the Lakshmi Narayan Temple. This temple is Delhi's major temple and is a popular tourist attraction. The temple is dedicated to the Lakshmi, the Goddess of wealth and to Lord Vishnu or one who preserves.

Address: Mandir Marg, Near Gole Market, Connaught Place, New Delhi, 110001

There are no fees to enter the temple. You will have to take your shoes off and like all religious places in India; there are stalls that will keep your shoes safe while you are in the temple. Cameras and mobile phones are not allowed in this temple. The best time to visit is during the aarti times or between 4:30 am to 1:30 pm and 2 pm to 9 pm.

The Birla Mandir also known as the Lakshmi Narayan
Temple

# Swaminarayan Akshardham Temple

This has to be one of the best temples I have seen. The temple showcases centuries of Hindu tradition, culture and history. It is said that 70% of tourists visiting Delhi visit the Swaminarayan Akshardham Temple. Situated on the Yamuna River, the temple has been crafted mostly of Rajasthani pink sandstone and Italian Carrara marble and no steel has been used. You cannot take any cameras, mobile phones or bags with you. You can hand them on a special counter which you can reclaim back after visiting the temple. Inside, the complex, it will take your breath away. It is absolutely magnificent. Inside the central dome there is a huge statue of Lord Swaminarayan (regarded as an incarnation of God). You will be able to buy vegetarian food inside the complex so you can time it in a way that you can have lunch there.

Address: Swaminarayan Akshardham, N. H. 24, Near Noida Mor, New Delhi 110092; Telephone: (011) 4344 2344

There are no fees and give yourself at least 2 to 3 hours to admire and complex. Entry to the complex is between 9.30 am to 6.30 pm and is closed on Mondays.

The central monument at Akshardham: <u>A Creative Commons picture</u> by <u>Swaminarayan Sanstha</u>

# Bahai Lotus Temple

Although 70% of the Indian people are Hindus, the Bahai religion has made a mark in India. They have constructed a temple called the Lotus Temple. This Bahai Lotus Temple is an architectural marvel. The temple was constructed by a Canadian architect Arthur Erickson and is regarded as an achievement of our time.

The temple is constructed in a 27-petaled shape, half-opened lotus and surrounded by beautiful lawns and nine pools and was opened to worshippers and the general public on the 24th of December 1986. Read more about the http://www.shalusharma.com/lotus-temple-must-see-bahai-temple.

You are not allowed to talk or take any photos when inside. Inside you will find benches all round and you can sit and admire the building or simply close your eyes and meditate. There are no fees to see this building. It's open all days of the week from 9 and to 7 pm in the summer and 9 am to 6 pm in winter.

Address: Lotus Temple Rd, Shambhu Dayal Bagh, Bahapur, New Delhi, 110019

The Lotus Bahai Temple from the outside

# Janpath Market

Janpath translates to People's Path in Hindi and is one of the major roads of Delhi. Located near Connaught Place, it is a must place to visit. Janpath market is a historical market and is popular amongst tourists and Indians alike. Basically, the market is full of shops, boutique stores and stalls that will cater for all pockets. You will also find touts selling stuff. You never know, you might like something – remember to bargain. Here's how to http://www.shalusharma.com/how-to-bargain-in-india.

You will find Indian handicrafts, clothes garments, jewellery, paintings, decorative items and much more. You can get souvenirs and gift items to take back home with you. There are plenty of food stores including western fast foods such as MacDonald's along with Indian ones.

Ask you are taxi or auto-driver to take you Janpath market. While you are there, you can also visit Connaught Place and Palika Bazaar (market).

Address: Janpath, New Delhi

One of the shops at Janpath Market

# Chandni Chowk

The Chandni Chowk area has one the ancient bazaars in Old Delhi. The market was established by the Mughal emperor Shah Jahan (the one who built the Taj Mahal) and designed by his daughter Jahanara in the 17th century. The place is very unusual and often dirty and can be congested and crowded with shoppers. You can buy anything under the sun at Chandni Chowk. Don't forget to bargain. If you don't want to buy anything, it's still worth visiting the market to experience the diverse culture of India. There are plenty of food stalls and restaurants for you to try. You can also visit the Jama Masjid (India's biggest mosque) while you are there.

Address: Chandni Chowk, Old Delhi, 110006. Just ask your driver to take you to the Chandni Chowk Market entrance. There is a Metro stop Chandni Chowk if you want to use the Metro.

One of the many streets of Chandni Chowk

# Jama Masjid

Although most of India's population are Hindus, India was ruled by Muslims for more than 1000 years that includes the powerful Mughals. The Jama Masjid or Mosque is a testimony of the architectural extravagance they indulged in. It is the largest mosque in India built by Shah Jahan in 1650-6 AD.

It is open for visitors from 7 am to Noon and then from 1.30 pm to 6.30 pm. You can hire an Islamic styled robe at the Northern Gate. Like all religious buildings in India, you will have to take your shoes off at the gate. The architecture is quite attractive but not as impressive as the ones you in see in Egypt and some of the medical buildings of Europe. But nonetheless, it has a great historical feel and ambience. You can hire a guide to take you around and explain the important of the numerous minarets and gates of the mosque.

You will need at least 1 to 2 hours to look around.

Address: Address: Chandni Chowk, Old Delhi; Phone: +91 11 2336 5358

Fees: Free entry but there is a 200 Rupees photography charge.

Jama Masjid in Old Delhi: Photo by <u>Rajarshi MITRA</u>, A <u>CC</u> Image

# Dilli Haat

The Dilli Haat is an open air bazaar for Indian handicrafts and items showing Indian culture, art and heritage. The place is set up by Delhi Tourism Department and the Handicrafts & handlooms association, Ministry of Textiles and the Ministry of Tourism of India. The sellers come from all over India on a rotational basis and set up their stalls and sell their authentic handicrafts. You will get the feel of rural India and the village market that still exists to this day. You will get to see lots of cultural activities as well. It's not just a market but a visual show of Indian culture and tradition. You will find lots of things and souvenirs for you to take back home. You will also find lots of excellent food stalls from all over India. It's certainly a very unique bazaar and a must a visit for the entire family. Read more about Dilli Haat here.

Address: There are two main Dilli Haats and a third one at Janakpuri.

Dilli Haat, INA, Shri Aurbindo Marg, Laxmi Bai Nagar, New Delhi
Phone: 011-26119055, 24678817

Dilli Haat, Pitam Pura (Near TV Tower), New Delhi, Ph: 011-27317663, 27310192

Hillary Rodham Clinton visiting the shops at Dilli Haat

# Jantar Mantar

These constructions where built by Maharaja Jai Singh of Jaipur in Delhi in the year 1724 for astronomical and astrological purposes. He built similar ones in Jaipur, Ujjain, Varanasi and Mathura meant for the compilation of astronomical tables, to predict movements of the sun, the moon and the planets. There are 3 instruments at the one in Delhi. The Samrat Yantra, to measure the declination and coordinates of various planets, the Jayaprakash Yantra to measure the alignment the position of a star and the third one called the Misra Yantra was a tool to figure out the shortest and longest days of the year. Those interested in the history of astronomy will find it fascinating. Find out more about the Jantar Mantar here.

Address: Sansad Marg, Connaught Place, New Delhi, 110001

Fees: 100 Rupees for foreigners

Jantar Mantar in Delhi

# Gali Paranthe Wali

While you are at the Chandni Chowk area of Delhi, make a point to visit the Gali Paranthe Wali, (lanes of paratha makers) a famous back street by lane for its parathas, the traditional Indian fried flat bread. It is one relic that has survived from the Mughal period; the lane is supposed to be about 300 years old.

You will find parathas and vegetable curries being sold in various stalls. These stalls in fact belong to the same family. The food is pure vegetarian with no onions or garlic used and since it has a high turnover, it is safe to eat. You can also try Indian sweets such as jalebis and drink lassi at the Gali Paranthe Wali. You might not be able to take your taxi or auto-rickshaw right up to the lane so ask your diver to take you as close as possible and ask your way up the lane. It is open from 9 am to 11 pm daily and the prices of these parathas are very cheap indeed.

Address: Paranthe Wali Gali, Maliwara, Maliwara Tiraha Bazar, Roshanpura, Old Delhi, 110006

Paratha shop at the Gali Paranthe Wali. Source:
Wildbindi. A CC image

# Safdarjung Tomb

The Safdarjung Tomb is a mausoleum made of marble and sandstone. The tomb was built in 1754 for Mirza Muqim Abul Mansur Khan known as Safdarjung, the Chief Minister of Awadh of the Mughal Empire. The tomb was the last one built by the Mughals.

Safdarjung Tomb is built in a lovely landscaped garden with wide foot paths and pools - an absolute pleasure to walk around. If you look carefully, it resembles Humayun's Tomb and the Taj Mahal but of lesser grandeur. The compound also encompasses a madrasa, an Islamic educational institute. You will need about an hour here to explore the tomb.

Address: Minto Road, Race Club, New Delhi. It is open all days of the week between 5 am to 7 pm.

Fees: Entry fees are 100 Rupees for foreigners.

The Safdarjung Tomb, the last tomb by the Mughals. A
<u>CC</u> image

# Rajpath

Rajpath is basically a straight road or ceremonial boulevard in New Delhi that connects the Presidents house on Raisina Hill and India Gate to National Stadium. You don't really need to do anything but just drive through it. You can simply ask the driver of your car, taxi or auto-rickshaw to take you there and just drive through it. You can stop and take some photos of course. You will see government buildings such as the Secretariat Building and the Parliament House of India. You can see the India gate and its surroundings and feels great to walk on the road. There are lots of greenery for you to walk around and admire the legacy of the British Empire. Rajpath is the creation of Lord Lutyan when the capital of British India was moved to Delhi.

The India Gate at one end of Rajpath. Image by Sebastien Rigault. A <u>CC</u> image

# Connaught Place

The Connaught Place or locally called CP is the financial centre of Delhi and a prominent business centre. It was named Connaught Place after the Duke of Connaught and made in Victorian architecture.

It's a very lively place and lots of tourists both Indian foreign visit this place. There are excellent shops, cinema halls (such as Rivoli, Odeon, Plaza, Regal) and restaurants all round and it will give you a feeling of being in an Eastern European country and at the same time enjoy what India has to offer. On the map of Delhi, you can see it as a big circle in the middle with lots of roads coming out from it. It's very close to the Janpath market and the famous Palika bazaar. You can simply stroll around for hours enjoying the shops and having cold coffee at the numerous stalls and restaurants. It's a great place for the whole family. The good thing is that many of the local attractions are close by.

Connaught Place is a great place to hang out. There are plenty of things to do

## Karol Bagh

Karol Bagh area of Delhi is famous for its markets that will cater for all pockets. If you visit this place then I suggest going in the evening time around 5 pm. You can spend the evening walking around getting entertained by the numerous street vendors, the touts and browsing the hundreds of shops. The main market is called Ghaffar Market. When you are fed up with walking or shopping around then simply have some street snacks or go to a place where you can have a quick snack like a chaat or anything else you fancy. There are plenty of these places and you won't have to look around where to eat. If you are looking for something Indian to wear then this is the place you can buy. Ask your driver to take you to the entrance of the market.

Shops lining the streets in Karol Bagh Market

# Final words

I hope you have enjoyed reading this mini ebook. I will reiterate that it was not a travel guide for Delhi but a list of places to see and visit on your trip to the capital of India. Delhi is one big historical city and you will need several days if you want to go through many of these listed places. But if you are in a hurry then you could spend a day or two just quickly going to these places and taking some pictures. And if you really liked something, you can always come back on another date for more.

The best modes of transport will be the auto-rickshaws as they are cheap and cheerful. Taxis are slightly expensive but more comfortable. Just make sure you go by the meter. Don't let the taxi drivers intimidate you or coax you into paying more.

You can always ask your hotel to organise you an air-conditioned cab to take you around these places. There are many organised tours of Delhi operated privately and by the Government of Delhi. Delhi Tourism also does tours at a reasonable price; however booking through them seems little odd and difficult to get through - you can check them out here. If you fill out this form on my website then you will get a suggest list of tour quotations and itinerary suggestions from several tour operators tailor made for you. You don't have to buy them but at least you will get a picture of the itineraries and pricing. You could organise a tour that consists of places in New Delhi and the next day you could go for monuments in Old Delhi or you could combine both together. You won't be able to see these places all in one day; you will need at least 2 to 3 days. Just decide what interests you the most. For a complete list of places to visit in Delhi, subscribe to my newsletter and get a copy of a free ebook comprising a complete list places to visit in Delhi.

Here's a list of other books that you might consider buying for your travels to India.

Find these books on amazon.com/author/shalusharma

Travel Guides

Essential India Travel Guide: Travel Tips And Practical Information
India Travel Survival Guide For Women
India Travel Health Guide: Health Advice and Tips for Travelers to India

Learn Hindi

Essential Hindi Words And Phrases For Travelers To India
Hindi Language For Kids And Beginners: Speak Hindi Instantly

For the kids

India For Kids: Amazing Facts About India
Mahatma Gandhi For Kids And Beginners
Life and Works of Aryabhata

Religion

Hinduism For Kids: Beliefs And Practices
Indian Religions For Kids
Religions of the World for Kids

Others

Real Ghost And Paranormal Stories From India

If you have any questions then feel free to email me on pyt@shalusharma.com or you can subscribe to my emails for updates, free books and deals here http://www.shalusharma.com/subscribe.

Thank you and enjoy your stay in Delhi

###

Printed in Great Britain
by Amazon